Caroline Arnold

BIRDS

Nature's Magnificent
Flying Machines

Illustrated by Patricia J. Wynne

ⅈ◔ⅈ Charlesbridge

To my husband Art who shares my
love of birds—C. A.

To my parents who loved watching
the geese fly south—P. W.

Eastern phoebes

Text copyright © 2003 by Caroline Arnold
Illustrations copyright © 2003 by Patricia J. Wynne
All rights reserved, including the right of reproduction in whole or in part in any
form. Charlesbridge and colophon are registered trademarks of Charlesbridge
Publishing, Inc.

Published by Charlesbridge
9 Galen Street
Watertown, MA 02472
(617) 926-0329
www.charlesbridge.com

Library of Congress Cataloging-in-Publication Data
Arnold, Caroline.
  Birds : nature's magnificent flying machines / Caroline Arnold ;
illustrated by Patricia J. Wynne.
      p. cm.
  Summary: An introduction to the science that explains how birds fly.
  ISBN 978-1-57091-516-1 (reinforced for library use)
  ISBN 978-1-57091-572-7 (softcover)
  ISBN 978-1-60734-207-6 (ebook pdf)
1. Birds—Flight—Juvenile literature. [1. Birds—Flight.] I. Wynne, Patricia J., ill.
II. Title.
QL698.7 .A76 2003
598—dc21   2002010441

Printed in Korea
(hc) 10 9 8 7 6 5 4 3
(sc) 15 14

Illustrations painted with colored inks and watercolor
Display type set in Elroy and text type set in Adobe Caslon
Color separations by P. Chan & Edward, Inc.
Printed by Sung In Printing in Gunpo-Si, Kyonggi-Do, Korea
Production supervision by Linda Jackson
Designed by Susan Mallory Sherman

Why Fly?

One spring day in 1804, when the great painter and naturalist John James Audubon was a teenager, he spied a pair of phoebes near his home in Pennsylvania. The birds were building a nest on a rocky ledge. Later, after the eggs in the nest hatched, Audubon watched the phoebes dart through the air catching insects to feed their hungry babies. The young birds grew fast and in a few weeks were ready to fly. They spread their wings, flapped, and flew a short distance. Audubon was amazed at how quickly they became experts, even though they had never flown before.

Almost all birds can fly. Flying helps birds find food, reach safe places for building nests, escape from predators on the ground, and travel easily over long distances. It helps them to survive.

Nature's Fliers

Birds, bats, and insects are the only groups of living animals that can fly. Of these, birds are by far the largest, fastest, and most powerful.

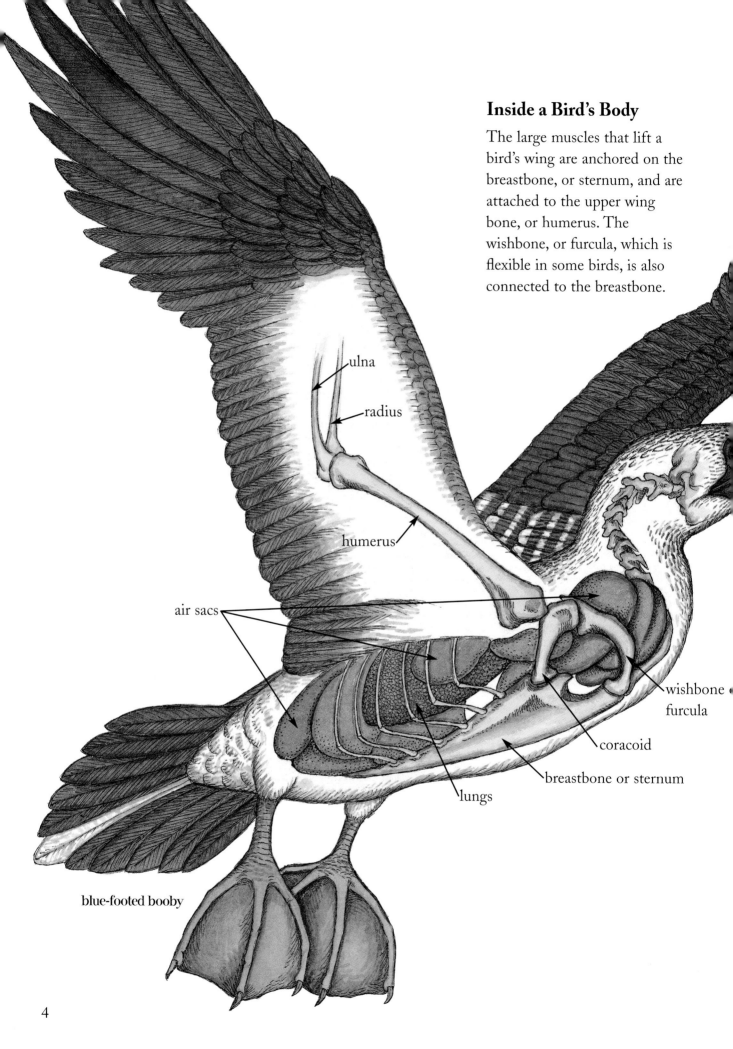

Inside a Bird's Body

The large muscles that lift a bird's wing are anchored on the breastbone, or sternum, and are attached to the upper wing bone, or humerus. The wishbone, or furcula, which is flexible in some birds, is also connected to the breastbone.

ulna

radius

humerus

air sacs

wishbone or furcula

coracoid

breastbone or sternum

lungs

blue-footed booby

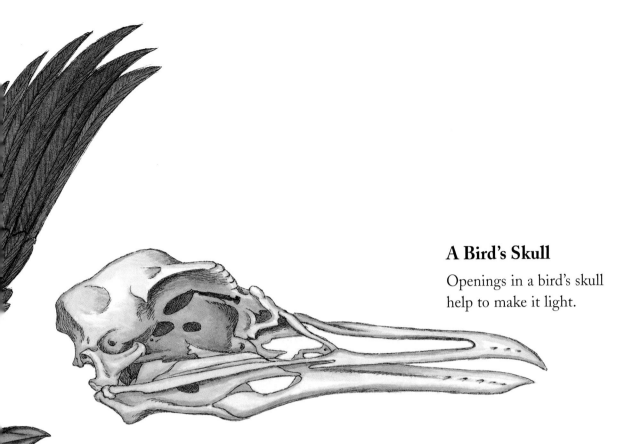

A Bird's Skull

Openings in a bird's skull
help to make it light.

Lightweights of the World

Lightweight bodies help birds to be good fliers.
If you jump off a chair, no matter how high you
jump or how hard you flap your arms, you land on
the floor. But when a bird takes off into the air, it
is so light it can overcome the pull of gravity.

A bird's skeleton is made of thin, hollow bones.
The skull is also thin and lightweight, and instead
of a heavy jaw with teeth, a bird has a much
lighter beak without teeth.

Another thing that makes a bird's body light is
a series of air sacs that fill spaces between other
organs. Most birds have nine air sacs. They are
connected to the lungs and help a bird to use more
of the air it takes in with each breath.

A Bird Bone Close-Up

If you cut a bird's bone
lengthwise, the inside looks
something like a
honeycomb. This network
of supports strengthens
the bone in the same way
that struts help support
a bridge.

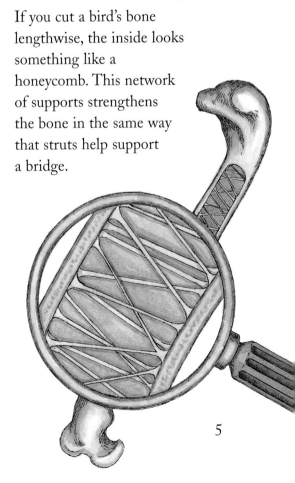

5

American flamingos

Designed for Flight

Birds need wings to fly. Look at a bird's wing from the side. It has a thick front edge and a downward curve toward the back. The distance over the top is greater than the distance across the bottom. When a bird moves through the sky, the air at the front of the wing separates as it flows over the wing's surface. The air traveling over the top goes faster than it does across the bottom. That's because it must go a longer distance in the same amount of time. The difference in airspeed causes a difference in air pressure. This pulls the wing at the top, pushes it from below, and creates a force called lift. Lift is what keeps a bird up in the air while it is flying.

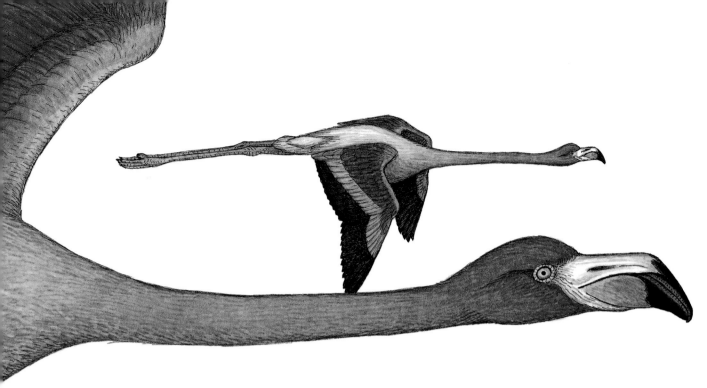

Lift

If you hold a piece of paper by one edge and blow across the top of it, you can see how lift is created. The faster-moving air on top of the paper pulls it up. Engineers use this principle when designing the wings of airplanes.

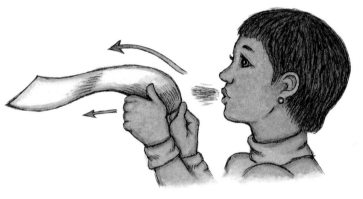

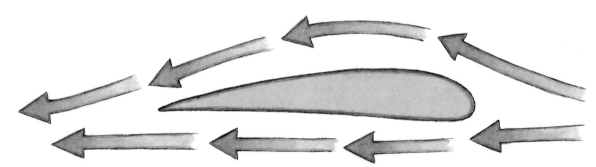

Creating Lift

The more quickly air moves over the top of the wings, the more lifting power they have. One way that a bird can increase its lifting power is by tilting its wings to increase their curve.

Feathers

Feathers are important for flying too. Long feathers on the wing, called flight feathers, make the wing bigger and give it shape. Tail feathers are used for steering. Short, smooth contour feathers cover the body and give it a streamlined shape. Short, fluffy down feathers lie next to the skin and help keep the bird warm.

Most feathers have a hollow center shaft with thin hairlike strands called barbs on either side. The barbs are connected to each other by tiny hooks called barbules. These help give a flight feather its smooth, airtight surface.

A Feather Close-Up

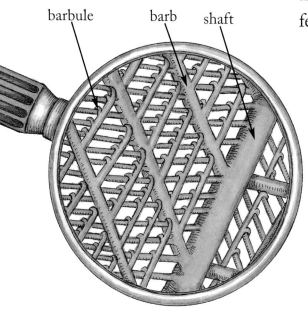

barbule   barb   shaft

Flight Feathers

On the shaft of a flight feather, the barbs on one side are longer than on the other.

Contour Feathers

Contour feathers are short and compact with barbs of equal length.

Down Feathers

Down feathers have no shaft. The silky fibers grow from a common point.

Temminck's tragopan (a pheasant)

Molting

Have you ever found a feather on the ground? Once a year, a few at a time, a bird's old feathers fall out and new feathers grow in. This process is called molting.

Wings

A bird's wings are its arms. The longest wing feathers, called primaries, are on the "hand." These provide the power for flight as the bird moves its wing down in the air. The secondary feathers are on the forearm and give the wing its curved shape. The shorter tertiary (TUR-shee-air-ee) feathers are on the upper arm and help make a smooth connection between the wing and body. Rows of short covert feathers go across the top of the wing and give it a curved edge.

The bones inside the wings are similar to those in your arm and hand. In the bird's hand, though, the finger bones are connected. This helps make the end of the wing strong. The thumb bone at the front of the wing is called the alula (AL-you-la). Feathers attached to the alula help direct the airflow across the wing so the bird does not stall, or fall, when it flies slowly.

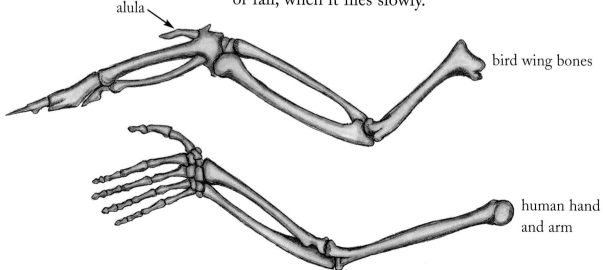

alula

bird wing bones

human hand and arm

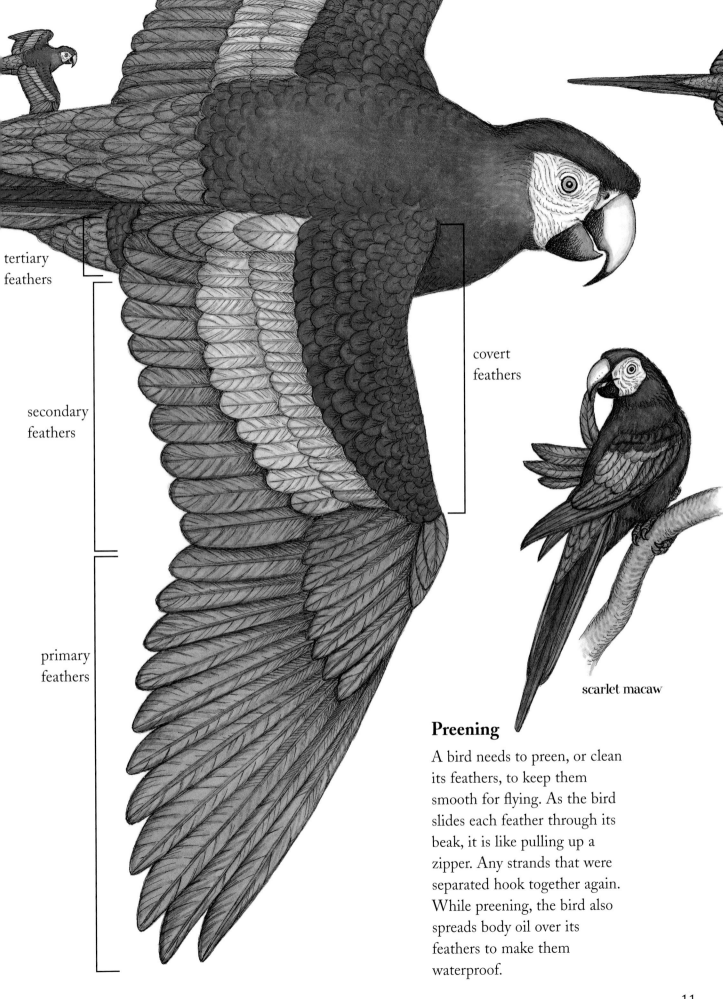

tertiary
feathers

secondary
feathers

primary
feathers

covert
feathers

scarlet macaw

Preening

A bird needs to preen, or clean
its feathers, to keep them
smooth for flying. As the bird
slides each feather through its
beak, it is like pulling up a
zipper. Any strands that were
separated hook together again.
While preening, the bird also
spreads body oil over its
feathers to make them
waterproof.

bald eagle

black-headed gull

Taking Off

Taking off from the ground is the hardest part of flying. A bird must flap its wings so fast that they will create enough airspeed to lift the bird into the air. This uses a great deal of energy. Whenever possible, a bird takes off facing the wind. The air blowing over the surface of the wings gives the bird a head start. Heavy birds have a harder time taking off than small birds do. A sparrow can fly right up into the air from a standing start. A gull, on the other hand, may have to run along the ground to gain enough speed for takeoff. Ducks paddle across the surface of the water to increase their takeoff speed. Herons bend their long legs and jump into the air. Eagles and vultures usually perch on cliffs or on the tops of tall trees. Up there they can spread their wide wings and catch the wind.

white-throated sparrow

black-crowned night heron

ruddy duck

Flapping

Flapping gives a bird the power to fly. As the ends of the wing move down through the air, they pull the bird forward. Air rushing over the wing lifts the bird in the air.

pintail duck

To begin flapping:

1. The bird lifts its wings high.
2. It moves the wings forward and down. The flat surface of the wing pushes the air like a broad paddle.
3. The downward motion is completed.
4. The bird lifts its wings back and up.
5. Now it opens the feathers like the slats on a window blind.
6. This helps air flow through them and makes it easier for the bird to raise its wings.
7. When they are fully lifted, the bird is ready to begin its next downward stroke.

4

5

6

7

Slow and Fast Flappers

Small birds flap faster than big birds do. Large birds, like vultures, flap about once a second. Medium size birds, like doves and crows, flap two or three times a second. Little birds, like chickadees, beat their wings about 30 times a second. A tiny hummingbird may flap its wings up to 80 times a second. That is so fast that the wings look like a blur.

ruby-throated hummingbird

black-capped chickadee

turkey vulture

white-winged dove

red-tailed hawk

wandering albatross

ruffed grouse

A Wing for Every Purpose

Each kind of bird has wings that are best for its way of life. Birds that spend most of their time on the ground often have short, rounded wings. This shape is good for darting and turning quickly. A grouse, for example, uses its powerful wings to fly up quickly when danger is near. Fast-flying birds usually have long, pointed wings. This shape is built for speed. Swallows and swifts flap their long wings as they chase insects in the air. Soaring birds have large wings for maximum lift. Birds that soar over the sea, such as albatrosses, usually have long, narrow wings that are good for riding with the wind. Birds that soar more slowly over land, such as hawks, have large, wide wings that are better for catching gentle breezes.

chimney swift

Night Fliers

An owl has soft feathers across the surface of its wings that muffle the noises made by flapping. This helps an owl approach its prey without being heard.

spotted owl

17

Thermals

If you see a bird soaring upward in circles, it is riding a thermal. A thermal is a column of warm air created by the uneven heating of the ground. The air spins as it rises. A thermal can quickly carry a bird up a mile or more in the sky. It is like an invisible elevator.

sharp-shinned hawk

Gliding and Soaring

Once a bird is in the air, it can often go for long distances without flapping at all. It simply spreads its wings and glides. The wings still provide lift while gliding, but without flapping, the bird will gradually sink to the ground.

The best gliders are birds with big wings. The broad surfaces of their wings provide a great deal of lift. Gulls, eagles, vultures, and albatrosses are all good gliders. An albatross can glide for miles.

Soaring is a type of gliding. Soaring birds use rising air currents to lift them into the air. Air rises when the sun heats the ground unevenly or when wind blows against the side of a mountain or building. Ocean birds soar on air currents made by wind blowing across the uneven surface of waves.

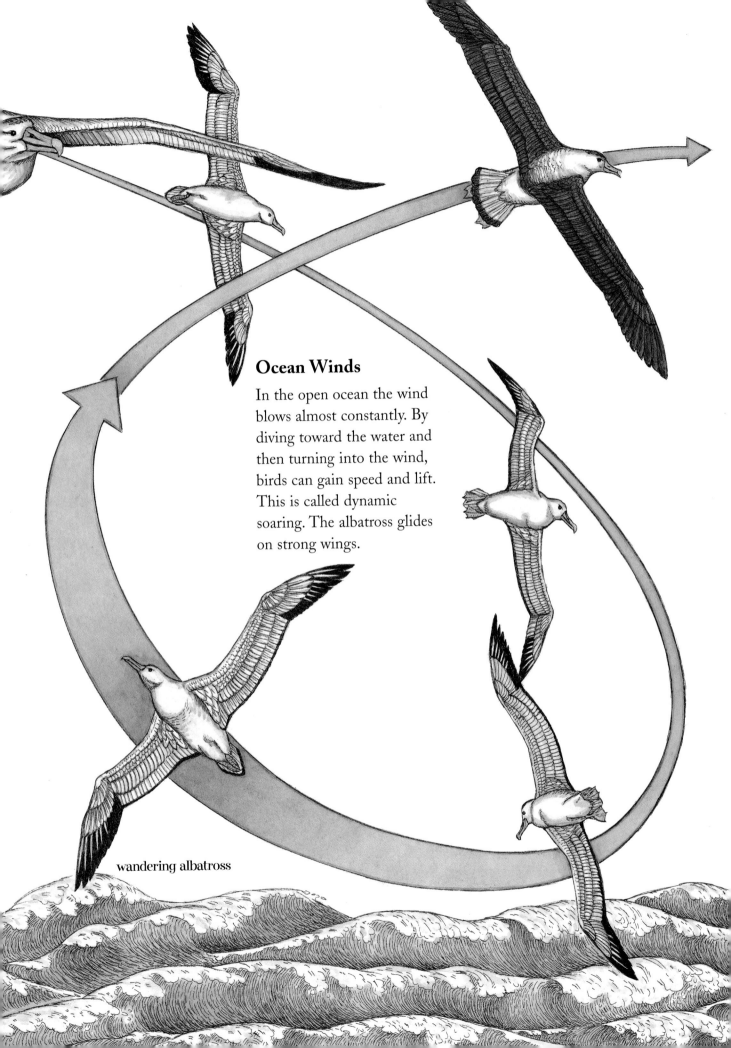

Ocean Winds

In the open ocean the wind blows almost constantly. By diving toward the water and then turning into the wind, birds can gain speed and lift. This is called dynamic soaring. The albatross glides on strong wings.

wandering albatross

American kestrel

Hovering

Have you ever watched a bird stay in one place while it flaps? It is hovering. Kestrels often hover as they search the ground for small animals. They flap their wings in a forward motion and tuck their tails underneath them as a brake. Most birds hover while facing into the wind. The wind blows them backward at the same rate that they are moving forward, so they stay still.

rufous hummingbird

Rivoli's hummingbird

broad-tailed hummingbird

Anna's hummingbird

The champions of hovering are the hummingbirds. These tiny birds can even fly backward for short distances. As the hummingbird hovers, it turns its body upward and flaps its thin, pointed wings. The wings turn at the shoulders so that the hummingbird gets lift on both the up and the down strokes.

Steering

Watch a bird to see how it changes its speed and direction as it flies. By raising or lowering its wings and twisting its tail, it can turn itself right or left. To move upward, the bird lifts its tail and lowers the back edge of its wings. To aim itself downward, the bird lowers its tail and raises the back edge of its wings. With what looks like little effort, the bird is able to control its movements exactly.

Young birds know how to fly without being taught. But they have to practice until they become experts at steering and landing.

cardinal

black-billed magpie

Landing

Landing is the most dangerous part of flying. If a bird lands too hard or fast, it could crash and hurt itself. If it comes in too slowly, it could miss the target.

All birds use their wings and tails as brakes to catch the air and slow their speed when landing. Birds such as magpies and crows, which land in trees, often approach a branch from below and then reach out with their feet to grab it. Birds such as seagulls, which land on the ground, often come to a running stop. Ducks, geese, and swans, like many waterbirds, hold their feet in front and skid across the top of the water as they land.

Ross' seagull

Long-Distance Fliers

Some birds stay in one place year-round. Others travel, or migrate, with the seasons. They migrate to find food, safe places for breeding, and better weather. Flying makes it possible for birds to cross natural barriers such as mountains, deserts, rivers, and oceans.

Many birds fly thousands of miles each year. Snow geese spend the summer in the Arctic. In the winter they fly as far south as Mexico. You can hear them honk as they fly overhead.

snow geese

Flying in Formation

Wild geese and ducks often fly in large V-shaped formations when they migrate. As each bird flaps its wings, it produces a swirl of rising air. The bird flying behind it can use this rising air to get extra lift. This helps it to save energy for the long journey. The birds take turns leading the group because that is the most tiring position.

The Long-Distance Champion

The Arctic tern has the longest known migration route. It flies 12,000 miles from the Arctic to the tip of South America.

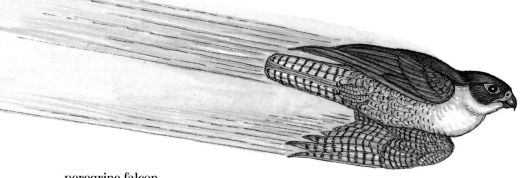
peregrine falcon

Fast Flyers, Slow Flyers, and No Flyers

The fastest known bird is the peregrine falcon. When diving for prey it can reach speeds of 200 miles per hour. In still air, most birds fly slower than 50 miles per hour. The average speed of a migrating hawk is about 30 miles per hour. The maximum speed of a ruby-throated hummingbird is 26 miles per hour. How fast a bird flies depends on the shape of its wings, as well as where it is going, and whether it is flying with or against the wind.

swallow-tailed kite

buff-bellied hummingbird

king penguin

ostrich

Some birds can't fly at all. They have other ways of surviving in the places where they live. Ostriches run on long, sturdy legs. Penguins use their paddle-shaped wings for swimming. The kiwi, which lives in the forests of New Zealand, hides from predators in burrows in the ground. So does the kakapo, a flightless New Zealand parrot.

kiwi

kakapo

Are Birds the Only Ones?

Birds are vertebrates, or animals with bony skeletons. The only other living vertebrates that can fly with powered wings are bats. Nearly 1,000 different kinds of bats live all over the world. Bats are night fliers, while most birds are active during the day.

A few other bony animals can glide in the air. They are not true fliers, but some can go long distances before landing. Gliders include flying fish, flying squirrels, flying frogs, and some snakes.

Pterosaurs

In dinosaur times there were flying reptiles called pterosaurs (TARE-o-sawrs). Some of them had wings 40 feet long from tip to tip. Pterosaurs are now extinct.

Bats

A bat's wings are formed by thin skin stretched between its body and the bones of its large hands.

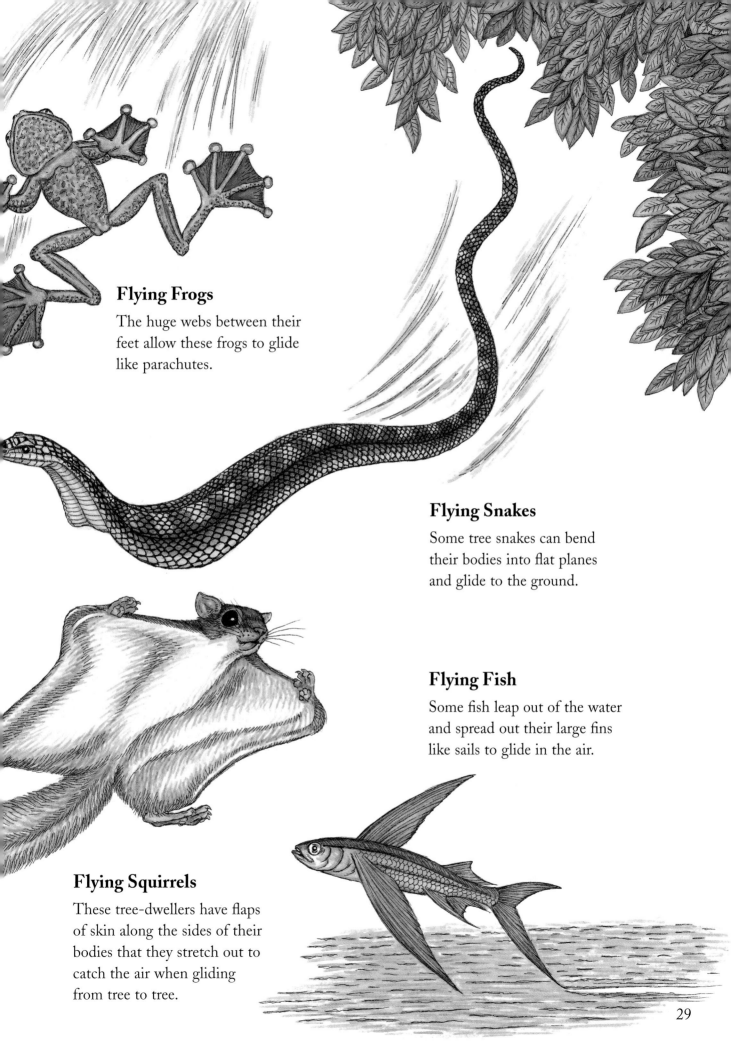

Flying Frogs

The huge webs between their feet allow these frogs to glide like parachutes.

Flying Snakes

Some tree snakes can bend their bodies into flat planes and glide to the ground.

Flying Fish

Some fish leap out of the water and spread out their large fins like sails to glide in the air.

Flying Squirrels

These tree-dwellers have flaps of skin along the sides of their bodies that they stretch out to catch the air when gliding from tree to tree.

Masters of the Air

The oldest known bird lived 150 million years ago during the age of the dinosaurs. Its name was *Archaeopteryx*. It had a tail and teeth like a reptile, but it flew on feathered wings. *Archaeopteryx* (ar-kee-OP-tuh-ricks) was not a strong flier, but over time its descendants became experts in the air.

Find the bird names on page 32

Mastery of the skies has allowed birds to live almost every place on Earth. Today there are nearly 10,000 species of birds. They have made their homes in places ranging from polar tundra to tropical forests, and from country fields to crowded cities. As we watch these aerial acrobats flit from branch to branch and soar in the sky above, we see how perfectly suited birds are to life in the air. They are truly magnificent flying machines.

snow geese

Glossary

alula—a group of small, stiff feathers attached to the thumb of a bird's wing

barbs—thin, hairlike strands that extend from the central shaft of a feather

barbules—tiny hooks that connect the barbs of a feather

contour feathers—large, stiff feathers that cover a bird's body

down feathers—small, fluffy feathers that form a warm undercoat in most birds

flight feathers—the long wing feathers that are used for flight; they are a type of contour feather

lift—the force that holds a bird or plane in the air

shaft—the stiff central part of a contour feather

stall—the sudden disappearance of lift caused by air swirling over the wing

thermals—large columns of rising air over the ground

vertebrates—animals with backbones

black-capped chi

Guides to Bird Identification

National Audubon Society. *Birds: First Field Guide*. New York: Scholastic, 1998.

Peterson, Roger Tory. *A Field Guide to the Birds* (Peterson Bird Guides). Boston: Houghton Mifflin Company, 2002.

Peterson, Roger Tory. *A Field Guide to Western Birds* (Peterson Field Guides). Boston: Houghton Mifflin Company, 1998.

Peterson, Roger Tory. *Birds* (Peterson First Guides). Boston: Houghton Mifflin Company, 1986.

Key for pages 30-31

1. yellow-billed cuckoo
2. whooping crane
3. European kingfisher
4. ruby-throated hummingbird
5. red-tailed hawk
6. barn swallow
7. osprey
8. scarlet ibis
9. *Archaeopteryx*
10. Ross' gull
11. rock dove
12. barn owl
13. Canada warbler
14. Atlantic puffin
15. Arctic tern
16. Gouldian finch
17. red-headed woodpecker
18 & 19. mallard ducks
20. American crow
21. black-crowned night heron
22. purple martin
23. Cuban tody
24. great gray owl